poet's fool's journeys
t. kilgore splake

front cover artwork by k carlton johnson

ISBN: 978-1-946460-49-3

poet's fool's journeys
t. kilgore splake

front cover artwork by k carlton johnson

Introduction
Dustin Pickering

The fool's journey is tricky and sometimes loaded, in every sense of the meaning. In these short poems of splake's, it seems that proverbial wisdom flies toward the Icarian sun to melt the snow laid down by God himself.

God too is the fool. In being the fool, God embraces the All—he sides with Creation. *Ein Sof* in the Kabbalistic tradition is the eternal of God, God before becoming manifest: thus, God originates in premeditated nothingness. Nothingness is something that circles back to us. In these short meditations, you will circle back frequently to new beginnings.

What is God but a being observing Himself? Consistently returning to the journey of the fool?

splake's original observations come from living the tricky life. Freedom is a pursuit, not an aim in itself. We do not look for freedom but it often finds us. Freedom embraces all things: beginning, end, and in-between. Freedom exists even in the negation of freedom since such negation is a choice, according to the fool.

The Tarot, like the I Ching, serves as a guide throughout the mishaps of a primal adventurer. I have known people who predicted events in their lives from these devices.

Sometimes we are clueless, indeed.

Poems are marks on the trail. These poems are intriguing, even illustrating that Nature herself is a fool constantly making and remaking things anew. The poet's task, in the modernist credo, is to 'make new'. However, these poems are curious in that they borrow from ancient modes of poeticizing. There's a little bit of tanka and haiku in the style. We might say that these forms, originating in parlor games, are also fool's pursuits, or journeys, in themselves. So to make anew sometimes you start from the beginning where the new originates. Rinse, wash, repeat…like a divorce, perhaps.

The fool's journey is one of constant remaking, constantly beginning again. Resurfacing into the beginning to find the newly adorned world.

I hope the reader finds pleasure in these fine words.

poet's fool's journeys

front cover artwork by k carlton johnson

poet's fool's journeys

r over forty-six years of my life, i was not aware of the quest of the tarot

rd fool. during that time i married, had sons and a daughter, lived in

burban house beautiful and practiced the free enterprise system with a

ars 'revolver credit card.

en early one morning, while nursing a hangover drinking a cup of black

ffee around the last night campfire coals, i wrote my first poem. it was

at surprised experience that revealed to me the wisdom of pursuing the

ot fool's continuous journeys.

e fool's journey represents a new beginning which requires ending your

d way of thinking and living. the great potential to pursue new adventures

d experience several different lives is to free oneself from the constraints

their past.

making this decision, i consciously divorced myself from my parent's

fluences, and no longer acted to please mother and father. also, as a free

man being, i denied relations to religious beliefs and political ideologies.

addition, while pursuing my fool's journey, i distanced myself from the

fluence of marriage and family structure, plus the community institutions

government and schools.

te: everyone has the potential to become a tarot fool, but very few possess

e intelligence and guts to play the fool's role. the tarot fool is a risk taker

d also a person unafraid of making mistakes. reflecting on my own personal history, the only people who succeed in gaining freedom for new lives and achieve a larger wholeness of themselves are those who have the courage to make fools of themselves along their journey.

# # # #

poet's fool's journeys

on life's endless adventure
traveling without beginning or end
after death disappearing in darkness

# # # #

another roadside attraction

finding old paperback in greyhound bus
discovering plucky purcell and highway zoo
jesus's corpse lost in torn out last pages

# # # #

shifu's wisdom

listening to wind
gentle wilderness music
whispering in dark pines

# # # #

non-buddha thinking

krzyewski and splake wisdom
not leaving ego at bard res' door
bringing best game to blank page

# # # #

arctic winter hell

black snowflakes falling
brutal minus zero windchill
ice and snow never melting

# # # #

suddenly spring

ice out snow gone
winter forest ghosts
dancing in wildflowers

# # # #

yooper spring morning

cooler air from overnight
light mist on lakes and streams
forest shadows disappearing in sun

# # # #

and yet

jennifer's soft blond hair
blowing in light forest breeze
brautigan's ghost whispering

# # # #

middle-age anatomy

viagra soft dick
sagging wrinkled scrotum
heart lost years ago

abortion

legs split lying on couch
staring at acoustical tiles
counting tiny dots

# # # #

honeymoon

harder deeper anxious sighs
woman desperate to go somewhere
soul has never been before

# # # #

junior high thesaurus

searching heart for right words
to shout love across empty page
fifteen year old's first romance

# # # #

little sparrow

dark paris basement bistro
eyes closed holding unlit cigarette
edith softly whispering "it's over"

\# \# \# \#

inspiration

poet suffering creative brain death
selling out his adversarial muse
begging god for divine revelation

\# \# \# \#

moving beyond

light evening forest breeze
dry tree leaves whispering
poet's ghost following path
deeper into wilderness

\# \# \# \#

reflections

destructive earthquakes and tornadoes
beyond our control of earth and sky
instead understand violence
enjoying nature's power
insignificance of who we are

# # # #

father's day

gray grizzled beard
worn leather biker vest
faded tattoos
warm smile on face
cold leinie's in each hand

# # # #

evening grace

home made potato soup
warming on hot plate
stravinsky's concert music
"rites of spring"
softly echoing in shadows

# # # #

talking with angels

poet's ghost returning

falling slowly to earth

in early morning raindrop

bringing fresh wisdom

after brief moment in heaven

communications

today cellphones

replacing personal diaries

now important to tell everyone

what used to be secrets

young girls no longer

having place to dream

# # # #

memories

ant farm worker
bee hive drones
slaves to routines
doing nothing creative
to leave after passing
proof to the world
they were here

# # # #

early morning existentials

poet welcoming daylight
through bloodshot eyes
brain throbbing
hands trembling
spilling cup of coffee
over felt-tipped pen
blank legal tablet page

# # # #

may morning

suddenly spring
ice out snow gone
wildflowers bursting from earth
white trillium blossoms
wilderness bouquet
while winter forest ghosts
dancing in dark shadows

\# \# \# \#

miracle

baby's first breath
tasting mother's milk
birth mysterious question
where life began
source of new soul
out of dark nothingness
before emerging from womb
crying into the world

\# \# \# \#

coming of age

young girls cellphones
snug in jeans back pockets
replacing personal diaries
no longer place
for telling special secrets
saving prom orchid
movie date ticket
photographs of friends
boyfriend's pubic hair

\# \# \# \#

graybeard reflection

contesting elusive muse
facing empty page
wondering if wasting time
better measure of success
attractive women grow old
sports cars wear out
can't hold wealth forever
while words remain
after poet's gone

\# \# \# \#

beyond wilderness

hiking deeper into woods
on rough narrow path
through thick tangled growth
leaving brautigan creek behind
quiet flowing waters
rippling over small rocks
fading musical whispers
echoing in early darkness
poet deer coyotes
waiting in moon shadows

# # # #

free at last

tranny-tripping early morning

battle creek city limits rearview mirror

steady hummm of tires on highway

poet heading true north

crossing mackinac bridge

returning to god's country

solitary traveler

imagination in high gear

dreaming of brook trout beauty

campfire cold beers

owls warm evening welcome

# # # #

elegy for li po

knapsack on back
full of haiku writings
wilderness pilgrim
hiking mountain paths
warming beside evening fire
sipping dinner wine
writing new poems
white-haired poet
drawing early winter breaths
as bright moon rising
above brautigan creek
knowing it is time

# # # #

father's presents

for birthdays and christmas
instead of toys and money
giving something with memories
for young son
compass and swiss army knife
thoreau's "walden" paperback
his daughter receiving
heavy rucksack and soft teddy bear
han shan's "cold mountain" poetry
native copper ring
after many years passing
dad's shadow forgotten
left important things
to shape children's lives

# # # # #

artistic dreams

young men early mornings
coffee shop breakfasts
before day's working hours
wives and babies home
marriage grown chilly
lost in empty lives
before divorces or death
boys growing up
without personal heroes
superman or john wayne
night's falling asleep
with sad thoughts
about not being creative
guys thinking
it could have been me

# # # #

seeing clearly now

sleepwalking through time
tenured college professor
hungry for something new
not sure just what
tired of always pretending
saying everything always okay
after thirty years teaching
life should make sense
still feeling just as lost
wasting many years
accumulating valuable things
driving expensive cars
secure investment savings
beautiful wives and lovers
society's idea of happiness
important to find myself
abandon big boy toys
phony academic prestige
finally breaking away
moving from
empty disappointing life

# # # #

www.ingramcontent.com/pod-product-compliance
Lightning Source LLC
Chambersburg PA
CBHW070801040426
42339CB00016B/462